Healthy Eating

Vegetables

Nancy Dickmann

www.raintreepublishers.co.uk
Visit our website to find out
more information about
Raintree books.

To order:
☎ Phone 0845 6044371
▤ Fax +44 (0) 1865 312263
▤ Email myorders@capstonepub.co.uk

Customers from outside the UK please telephone +44 1865 312262

Raintree is an imprint of Capstone Global Library Limited, a company incorporated in England and Wales having its registered office at 7 Pilgrim Street, London, EC4V 6LB – Registered company number: 6695582

"Raintree" is a registered trademark of Pearson Education Limited, under licence to Capstone Global Library Limited

Edited by Siân Smith, Nancy Dickmann, and Rebecca Rissman
Designed by Joanna Hinton-Malivoire
Picture research by Elizabeth Alexander
Production by Victoria Fitzgerald
Originated by Capstone Global Library Ltd
Printed and bound in China by South China Printing Company Ltd

ISBN 978 0 431 00549 2
14 13 12 11 10
10 9 8 7 6 5 4 3 2 1

British Library Cataloguing in Publication Data
Dickmann, Nancy.
  Vegetables. -- (Healthy eating)
  1. Vegetables--Juvenile literature. 2. Vegetables in human nutrition--Juvenile literature.
  I. Title II. Series
  641.3'5-dc22

Acknowledgements
We would like to thank the following for permission to reproduce photographs: © Capstone Publishers pp.**16**, **22** (Karon Dubke); Alamy pp.**20**, **23 middle** (© MBI); Corbis pp.**10** (© amanaimages), **21** (© Gideon Mendel); Food Standards Agency/ © Crown copyright material is reproduced with the permission of the Controller of HMSO and Queen's Printer for Scotland p.**19**; Getty Images p.**17** (Robert Daly/OJO Images); iStockphoto pp.**4**, **23 bottom** (© Dana Bartekoske), **7** (© David T. Gomez), **8** (© Shane Cummins), **11** (© Jon Faulknor), **14** (© Doug Schneider), **15** (© Francisco Romero), **23 top** (© Mark Hatfield); Photolibrary pp.**5** (Image Source), **6** (Mode Images), **12** (OJO Images/Andrew Olney), **13** (Jasper James); Shutterstock pp.**9** (© Elena Kalistratova), **18** (© Monkey Business Images).

Front cover photograph of vegetables reproduced with permission of © Capstone Publishers (Karon Dubke). Back cover photograph reproduced with permission of iStockphoto (© Doug Schneider).

We would like to thank Dr Sarah Schenker for her invaluable help in the preparation of this book.

Every effort has been made to contact copyright holders of material reproduced in this book. Any omissions will be rectified in subsequent printings if notice is given to the publishers.

Contents

What are vegetables?

A vegetable is a type of plant we eat.

Eating vegetables can keep
us healthy.

carrot

Some vegetables grow under the ground.

peas

Some vegetables grow above the ground.

Looking at vegetables

onion

Some vegetables are short
and round.

bean

Some vegetables are long and thin.

Many vegetables are green.

beetroot

carrot

Some vegetables are orange
or purple.

How vegetables help us

Vegetables are full of nutrients.

You need nutrients to stay healthy.

Eating carrots helps keep your skin and eyes healthy.

Eating spinach helps keep your
blood healthy.

Eating sweet potatoes gives
you energy.

You need energy to work and play.

Healthy eating

We need to eat five servings of fruit and vegetables each day.

fruit and vegetables

The eatwell plate shows us which foods to eat.

We eat vegetables to stay healthy.

We eat vegetables because they taste good!

Find the vegetable

Here is a healthy dinner. Can you find two vegetables?

Answer on page 24

Picture glossary

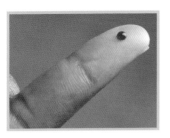

blood red liquid inside your body. Blood takes food and air to all your body parts.

energy the power to do something. We need energy when we work or play.

nutrients things our bodies need to stay healthy. You can get nutrients in different foods.

Index

Answer to quiz on page 22: The two vegetables are carrots and broccoli.

Notes for parents and teachers

Before reading

Explain that we need to eat a range of different foods to stay healthy. Splitting foods into different groups can help us understand how much food we should eat from each group. Introduce the fruit and vegetables group. How many different vegetables can the children think of? Explain that eating five portions of fruits and vegetables every day can help us to stay healthy.

After reading

• Choose children to mime some benefits of eating vegetables for the others to guess. These can include keeping our skin, teeth, and gums healthy; building strong muscles; healing cuts and bruises; fighting illnesses; helping us see in the dark; helping us to digest food and get rid of waste products.

• Create a bar chart or pictogram with the children to show the different vegetables they have eaten or tasted over the course of a week. Make it a challenge to see how high you can get the bar for each vegetable to go, and to see if you can add new vegetables to the chart.

• Ask the children to bring in pictures of as many different vegetables as they can find. Divide the children into groups and ask the groups to explore different ways of sorting the vegetables. For example, they might sort them by shape, size, colour, preference, or whether they can be eaten raw. Collages of grouped vegetables can be put up on the wall.